1

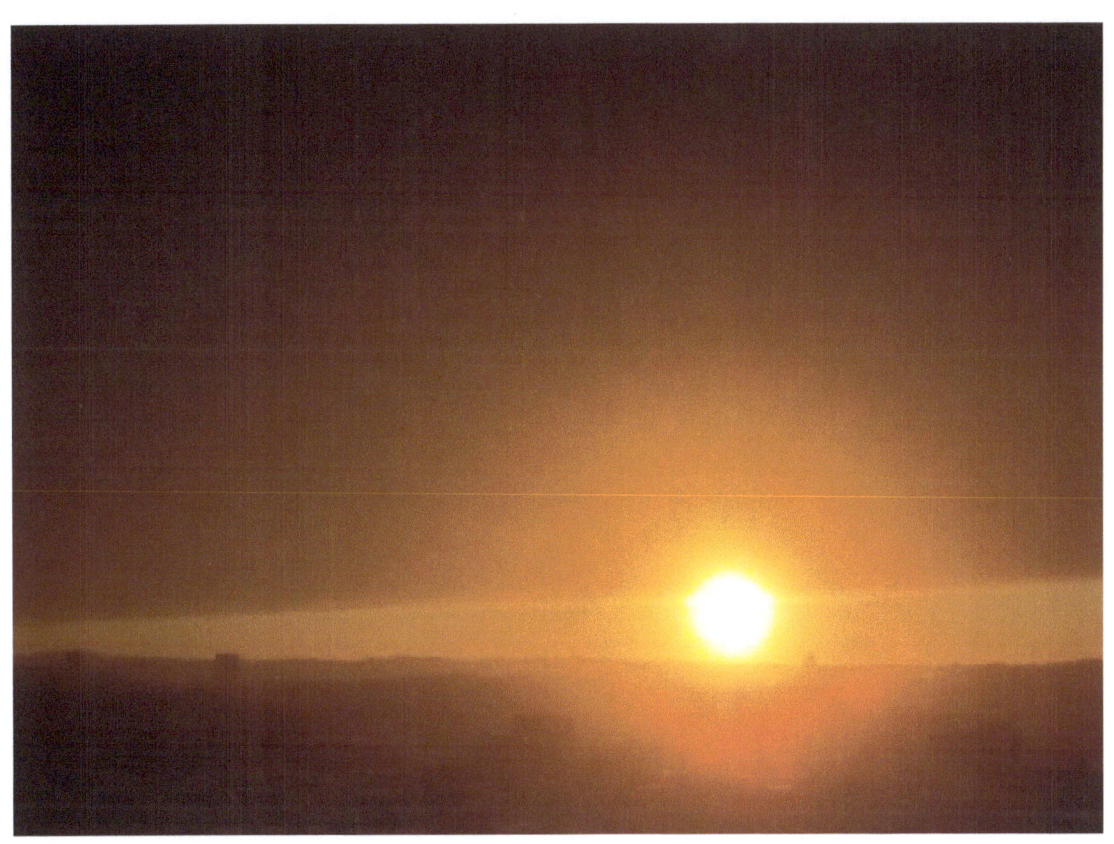

SUNSETS

By Jose Diaz

Artwork Copyright © 2013 **José Diaz**
ISBN-13:
978-1523937912

ISBN-10:
1523937912

Published by Long Time Ago Books
Editor: William Russo

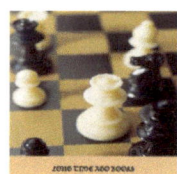

LONG TIME AGO BOOKS

TABLE OF CONTENTS

Foreword by Dr. William Russo
Press Release
In My Own Words by Jose Diaz

POEMS

ABOUT THE AUTHOR

FOREWORD

Diaz is a supernova.

Nearly two decades ago, I met artist José Diaz. He seemed like an urchin, exemplifying the environment of parental absence, institutional living, and having no one to encourage artistic development that had many adolescent artists in Brockton, Massachusetts.

As a young adult, José showed me several of his art works that he did alone, seldom sharing. I was astounded because I had never seen complex images done completely by colored pencils.

During his lonely days as a child, between school and visiting his mother as she came to her final rest in a hospital, he took to making little drawings of clouds. When I met him, many of his pencils, expensive to buy when you have no money, had become nubs in his hands.

He had never attended an art class and had been neglected in the public schools. Yet, here too was another innate talent, refusing to be overshadowed by the apathy of the world around him.

José lived through many traumas, many part-time jobs to keep his life going, but through it all he kept at his artwork, which was for him both a respite and a sanctuary. Most people to whom he showed his work were puzzled by its uniqueness.

Only after perseverance and community art shows in places like Jamaica Plain, Massachusetts, José did start to realize there were people who were astounded by his work and others who found his work so original that he did not fit in community shows.

Around the time of the Hubble telescope photos, he took to drawing the night sky with *aurora borealis* and more. Original Hubble photos were actually recreations of numerical patterns, and his work was truly art imagined.

  Diaz came out of Brockton, Mass., the city better known for Rocky Marciano and Marvelous Marvin Hagler, boxers who fought to be champions.   José Diaz has fought no less--and fought harder to reach his artistic goals.

Long Time Ago Books is delighted to have the chance to showcase the extraordinary talent of this artist, similar to seers and mystics in their sixth sense, to the greater public.

This latest volume features Jose's photography, selecting images as an emblem of his soul. No filters or other devices are used. What you see is what he sees.

Mr. Diaz has selected some of his favorite classic poems and poets who have also touched on the subject of sunsets. There is more here than meets the eye.

Dr. William Russo
Editor, Long Time Ago Books

Press Release of *Arte Galeria de Enid*
Rincon, Puerto Rico, 2012

Diaz has studied art for as long as he can remember.

Born in New York City of parents from Puerto Rico, José Diaz suffered a traumatic childhood when his parents died while he was a boy. He found consolation and happiness in drawing pictures.

After his tragic losses, he stayed with a series of foster homes where he took his only comfort in making pictures with colored pencils in free-hand style. He worked endlessly on his gift to hone the ability to create without ever having any art courses or lessons. He is self-taught and creates artwork that his heart tells him.

He kept those pencils for many years, drawing till they were nubs, but by then he had honed his special gift for landscapes that feature clouds and celestial drawings that rival Hubble telescope pictures.

Photos from Hubble gave José a spiritual sense, and they inspired him to draw his stunning celestial works of the heavens. He also found the *Aurora Borealis* an important influence on him. Images of sky and clouds are another consistent motif in his work.

These three ideas are powerful symbols in Jose's artwork. They remain the most important images in all his creative efforts.

His extraordinarily detailed colored pencil work, whether of seashores or galaxies, astounds viewers and art critics with their delicacy of form and ability to create a sense of peace and awe.

José also enjoys the shape and colors of tropical plants that remind him of childhood visits to Puerto Rico, and he tries to capture their beauty and delicacy in all his drawings.

For many years, José lived in and around Boston, Massachusetts, with his longhaired Chihuahua.

Today he happily continues to draw unique and special works that express spiritual connections to the universe and to eternity. His photographs are another expression of that spirituality.

IN MY OWN WORDS

When I was eleven years old, I used crayons to draw pictures. I would make my own images of trees and little designs. It was a hobby that allowed me to be creative and feel a bit of satisfaction about my drawings.

No one ever encouraged me. My mother was artistic and started as a girl by drawing fashion pictures, but she was busy with her business when I started drawing at 11 and 12 years of age. Later, she became extremely ill and never had a chance to see any of my fully developed artistic efforts.

I took an art class in high school, but no one was working with the medium of colored pencils. So, I could find no teachers to help me with the direction of my earliest art. A few instructors saw my work and simply told me to draw what I feel, and I remained independent and outside regular classes of art.

There was no role model for me in terms of artists. There was no artist whose example I could find who was doing anything with colored pencils. So, I simply drew foliage and trees with leaves on my own. I experimented with designs and small objects. It was a completely self-taught experience. My work was private, really shared with no one for the first few years.

I bought supplies for my art by shoveling snow after big storms in Brockton, Mass., where I lived. I would get enough money to buy some expensive supplies.

By the time I was 18, I became interested in tropical scenes, like beaches in Puerto Rico and Cape Cod. I always found the beach and sand and sky meeting to be magical, a stress reducer, and a cleansing experience.

Later I put my focus on drawing the complexities of clouds, which I found to be the perfect spiritual symbols.

My work became more ambitious, inspired by science television shows that dealt with astronomy and meteorology. Later the images from the Hubble telescope gave me an appreciation of the Earth's fragility.

Another influence upon my work has been New Age music that often keeps my mind in focus as I sit at the drawing board. I experimented often with acrylics, but found that were not disciplined enough for my purposes. They were messy and not exact. I prefer detail work, designs that I find in landscapes, clouds, and leaves of trees. I find the blade of grass to be a fascinating detail to draw.

My work requires hours of concentration. Once I begin a work, I seldom take much more than a few minutes of a break once in a while. I will go without sleep and work all day until the picture is complete. It takes two days to do a small effort, and upwards of two to three weeks for the larger pieces. I work because I need to finish before I can move on with anything in life.

In recent years I turned to drawing the Northern Lights or the Auroras on black paper. The focus on the universe provides special perspective on the delicacy of life on Earth. I have found that the pieces on the universe have taught me that life is delicate and that nature is ephemeral. Yes, the Earth is like a blue glass sphere that will shatter into a million pieces. If that happens, the universe will simply continue without us. The universe has no sympathy for humanity.

The modern world of art has moved into computer-generated art that I think may be better used for fashion, engineering, or architecture.

In ten years I hope to work into other styles, perhaps abstracts or some version of acrylic and oils mixed on a canvas. The heart of an artist hinges on experiments with his work. That's how I started, and it is how I will continue to work in the future.

Sincerely,

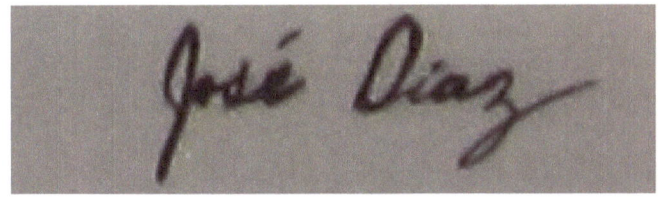

José Diaz

Song at Sunset by Walt Whitman

SPLENDOR of ended day, floating and filling me!
Hour prophetic—hour resuming the past!
Inflating my throat—you, divine average!
You, Earth and Life, till the last ray gleams, I sing.

Open mouth of my Soul, uttering gladness,
Eyes of my Soul, seeing perfection,

Natural life of me, faithfully praising things;
Corroborating forever the triumph of things.

Illustrious every one!
Illustrious what we name space—sphere of unnumber'd spirits;
Illustrious the mystery of motion, in all beings, even the tiniest insect;
Illustrious the attribute of speech—the senses—the body;
Illustrious the passing light! Illustrious the pale reflection on the new
moon in the
western
sky!
Illustrious whatever I see, or hear, or touch, to the last.

Good in all,
In the satisfaction and aplomb of animals,
In the annual return of the seasons,
In the hilarity of youth,
In the strength and flush of manhood,
In the grandeur and exquisiteness of old age,
In the superb vistas of Death.

Wonderful to depart;
Wonderful to be here!
The heart, to jet the all-alike and innocent blood!
To breathe the air, how delicious!
To speak! to walk! to seize something by the hand!
To prepare for sleep, for bed—to look on my rose-color'd flesh;
To be conscious of my body, so satisfied, so large;
To be this incredible God I am;
To have gone forth among other Gods—these men and women I love.

Wonderful how I celebrate you and myself!
How my thoughts play subtly at the spectacles around!
How the clouds pass silently overhead!
How the earth darts on and on! and how the sun, moon, stars, dart on
and on!
How the water sports and sings! (Surely it is alive!)
How the trees rise and stand up—with strong trunks—with branches
and leaves!
(Surely there is something more in each of the tree—some living Soul.
)

O amazement of things! even the least particle!
O spirituality of things!
O strain musical, flowing through ages and continents—now reaching me and America!
I take your strong chords—I intersperse them, and cheerfully pass them forward.

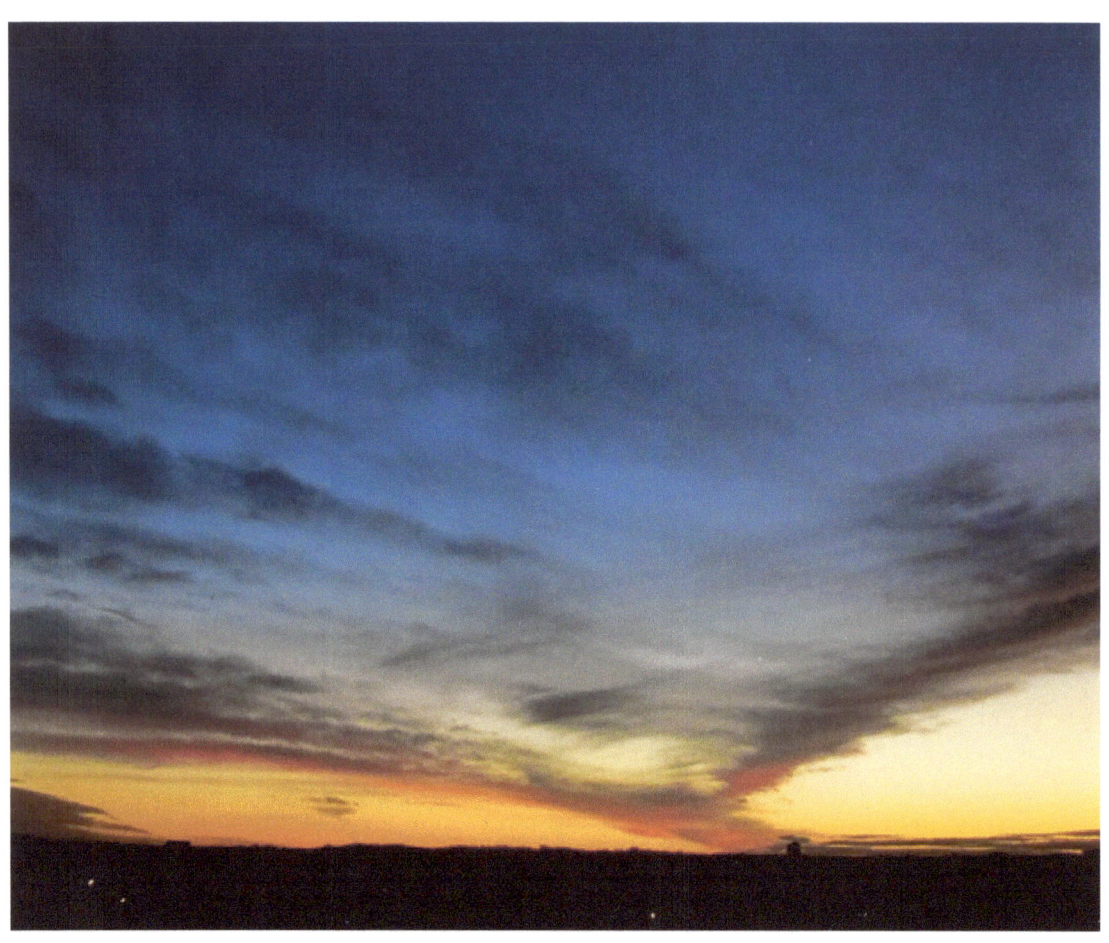

I too carol the sun, usher'd, or at noon, or, as now, setting,
I too throb to the brain and beauty of the earth, and of all the growths of the earth,
I too have felt the resistless call of myself.

As I sail'd down the Mississippi,
As I wander'd over the prairies,

As I have lived—As I have look'd through my windows, my eyes,
As I went forth in the morning—As I beheld the light breaking in the
east;
As I bathed on the beach of the Eastern Sea, and again on the beach
of the Western Sea;
As I roam'd the streets of inland Chicago—whatever streets I have
roam'd;
Or cities, or silent woods, or peace, or even amid the sights of war;
Wherever I have been, I have charged myself with contentment and
triumph.

I sing the Equalities, modern or old,
I sing the endless finales of things;
I say Nature continues—Glory continues;
I praise with electric voice;
For I do not see one imperfection in the universe;
And I do not see one cause or result lamentable at last in the
universe.

O setting sun! though the time has come,
I still warble under you, if none else does, unmitigated adoration.

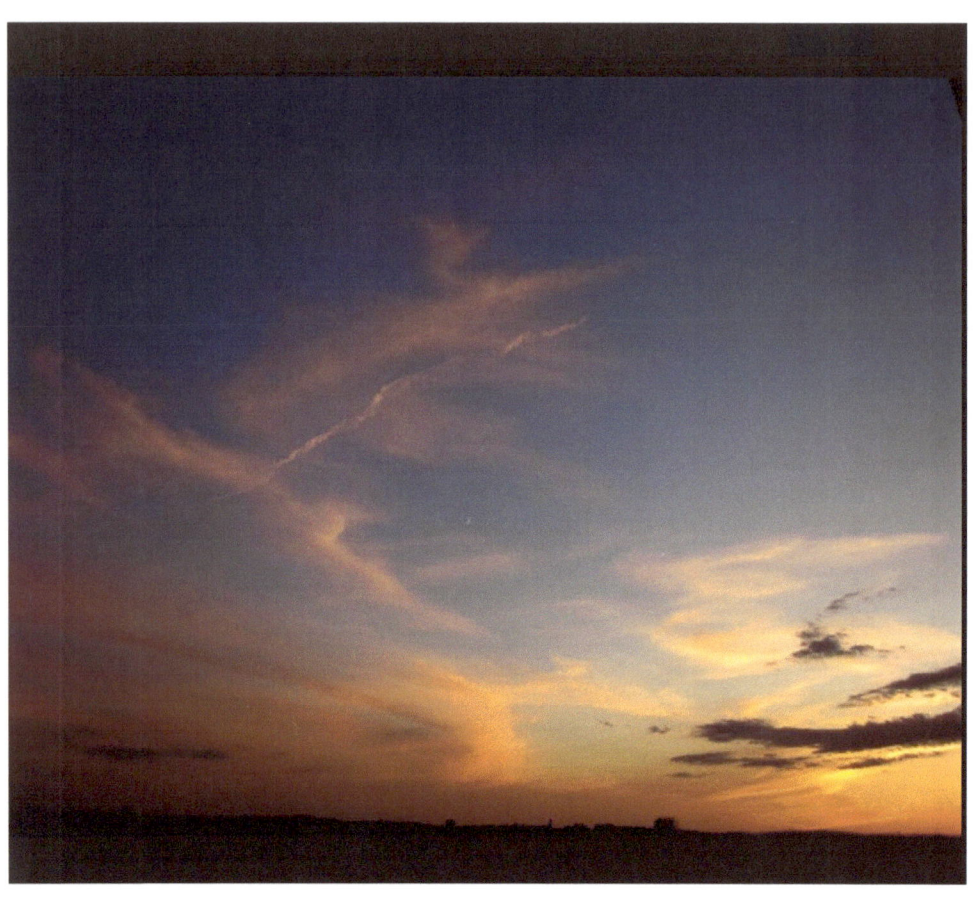

A Sunset by Victor Hugo

  I love the evenings, passionless and fair, I love the evens,
Whether old manor-fronts their ray with golden fulgence leavens,
In numerous leafage bosomed close;
Whether the mist in reefs of fire extend its reaches sheer,
Or a hundred sunbeams splinter in an azure atmosphere
On cloudy archipelagos.

Oh, gaze ye on the firmament! a hundred clouds in motion,
Up-piled in the immense sublime beneath the winds' commotion,
Their unimagined shapes accord:
Under their waves at intervals flame a pale levin through,
As if some giant of the air amid the vapors drew
A sudden elemental sword.

The sun at bay with splendid thrusts still keeps the sullen fold;
And momently at distance sets, as a cupola of gold,
The thatched roof of a cot a-glance;
Or on the blurred horizon joins his battle with the haze;
Or pools the blooming fields about with inter-isolate blaze,
Great moveless meres of radiance.

Then mark you how there hangs athwart the firmament's swept track,
Yonder a mighty crocodile with vast irradiant back,
A triple row of pointed teeth?
Under its burnished belly slips a ray of eventide,
The flickerings of a hundred glowing clouds in tenebrous side
With scales of golden mail ensheathe.

Then mounts a palace, then the air vibrates--the vision flees.

Confounded to its base, the fearful cloudy edifice
Ruins immense in mounded wrack;
Afar the fragments strew the sky, and each envermeiled cone
Hangeth, peak downward, overhead, like mountains overthrown
When the earthquake heaves its hugy back.

These vapors, with their leaden, golden, iron, bronzèd glows,
Where the hurricane, the waterspout, thunder, and hell repose,
Muttering hoarse dreams of destined harms,--
'Tis God who hangs their multitude amid the skiey deep,
As a warrior that suspendeth from the roof-tree of his keep
His dreadful and resounding arms!

All vanishes! The Sun, from topmost heaven precipitated,
Like a globe of iron which is tossed back fiery red
Into the furnace stirred to fume,
Shocking the cloudy surges, plashed from its impetuous ire,
Even to the zenith spattereth in a flecking scud of fire
The vaporous and inflamèd spaume.

O contemplate the heavens! Whenas the vein-drawn day dies pale,
In every season, every place, gaze through their every veil?
With love that has not speech for need!
Beneath their solemn beauty is a mystery infinite:

If winter hue them like a pall, or if the summer night
Fantasy them starre brede.

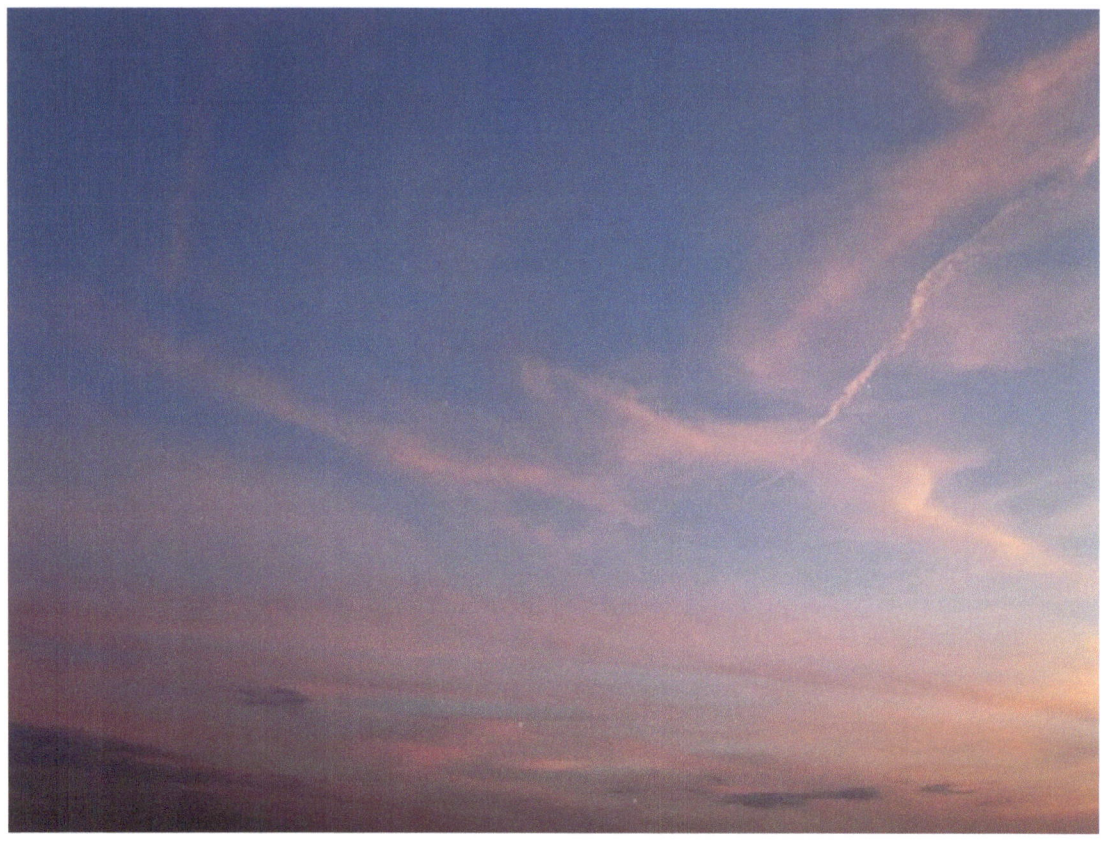

The Negro Speaks of Rivers by Langston Hughes

I've known rivers:
I've known rivers ancient as the world and older than the
flow of human blood in human veins.

My soul has grown deep like the rivers.

I bathed in the Euphrates when dawns were young.

I built my hut near the Congo and it lulled me to sleep.

I looked upon the Nile and raised the pyramids above it.

I heard the singing of the Mississippi when Abe Lincoln
 went down to New Orleans, and I've seen its muddy
 bosom turn all golden in the sunset.

I've known rivers:
Ancient, dusky rivers.

My soul has grown deep like the rivers.

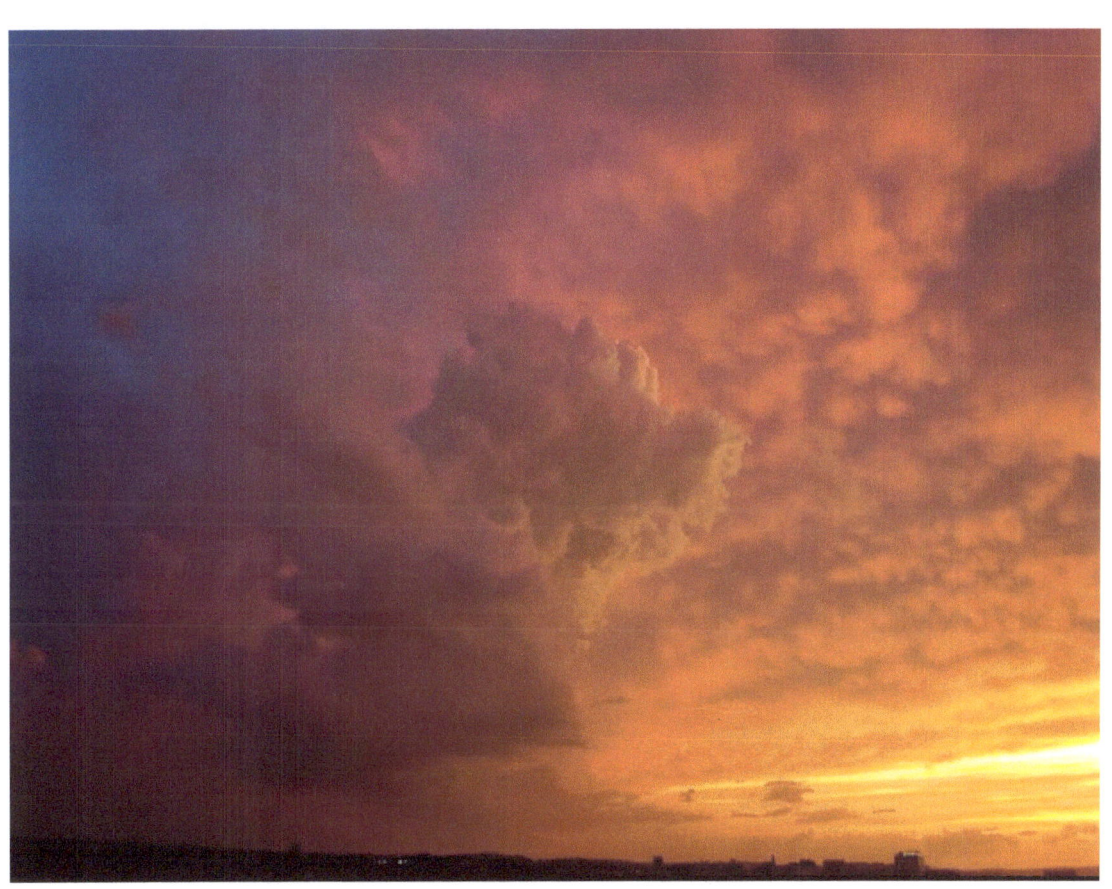

The Pumpkin by John Greenleaf Whittier

Oh, greenly and fair in the lands of the sun,

The vines of the gourd and the rich melon run,
And the rock and the tree and the cottage enfold,
With broad leaves all greenness and blossoms all gold,
Like that which o'er Nineveh's prophet once grew,
While he waited to know that his warning was true,
And longed for the storm-cloud, and listened in vain
For the rush of the whirlwind and red fire-rain.

On the banks of the Xenil the dark Spanish maiden
Comes up with the fruit of the tangled vine laden;
And the Creole of Cuba laughs out to behold
Through orange-leaves shining the broad spheres of gold;
Yet with dearer delight from his home in the North,
On the fields of his harvest the Yankee looks forth,
Where crook-necks are coiling and yellow fruit shines,
And the sun of September melts down on his vines.

Ah! on Thanksgiving day, when from East and from West,
From North and from South comes the pilgrim and guest;
When the gray-haired New Englander sees round his board
The old broken links of affection restored;
When the care-wearied man seeks his mother once more,
And the worn matron smiles where the girl smiled before;
What moistens the lip and what brightens the eye,
What calls back the past, like the rich Pumpkin pie?

Oh, fruit loved of boyhood! the old days recalling,
When wood-grapes were purpling and brown nuts were falling!
When wild, ugly faces we carved in its skin,
Glaring out through the dark with a candle within!
When we laughed round the corn-heap, with hearts all in tune,
Our chair a broad pumpkin, -- our lantern the moon,
Telling tales of the fairy who travelled like steam
In a pumpkin-shell coach, with two rats for her team!

Then thanks for thy present! none sweeter or better
E'er smoked from an oven or circled a platter!
Fairer hands never wrought at a pastry more fine,
Brighter eyes never watched o'er its baking, than thine!
And the prayer, which my mouth is too full to express,
Swells my heart that thy shadow may never be less,
That the days of thy lot may be lengthened below,
And the fame of thy worth like a pumpkin-vine grow,

And thy life be as sweet, and its last sunset sky
Golden-tinted and fair as thy own Pumpkin pie!

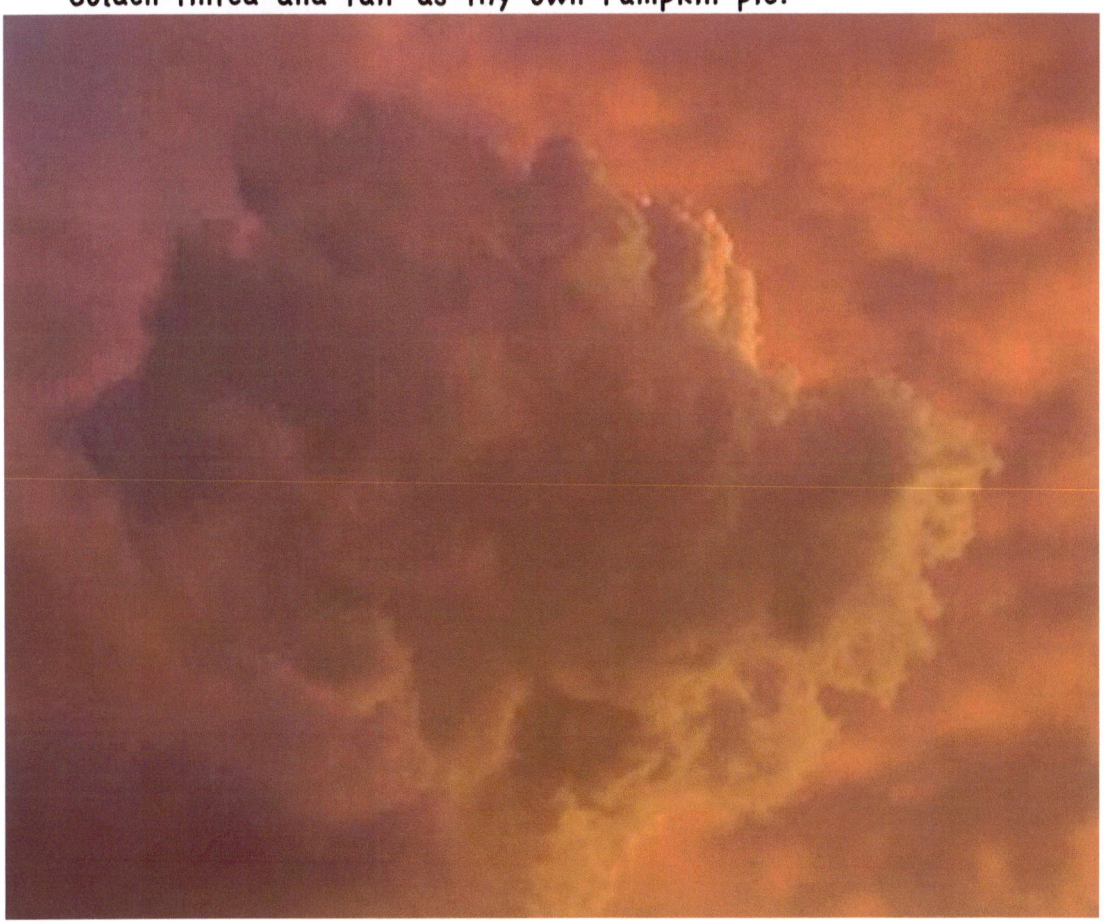

An Autumn Sunset by Edith Wharton

I

Leaguered in fire
The wild black promontories of the coast extend
Their savage silhouettes;
The sun in universal carnage sets,
And, halting higher,
The motionless storm-clouds mass their sullen threats,
Like an advancing mob in sword-points penned,
That, balked, yet stands at bay.

Mid-zenith hangs the fascinated day

In wind-lustrated hollows crystalline,
A wan Valkyrie whose wide pinions shine
Across the ensanguined ruins of the fray,
And in her hand swings high o'erhead,
Above the waste of war,
The silver torch-light of the evening star
Wherewith to search the faces of the dead.

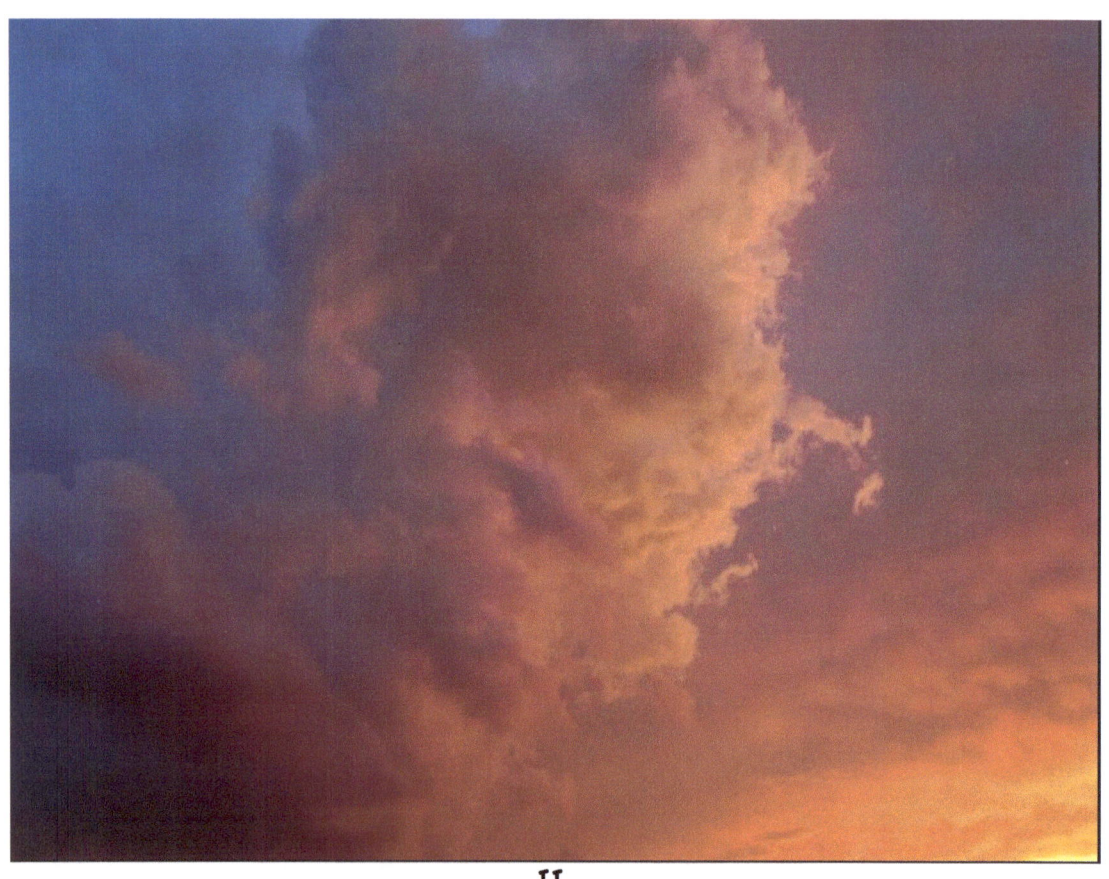

II

Lagooned in gold,
Seem not those jetty promontories rather
The outposts of some ancient land forlorn,
Uncomforted of morn, Where old oblivions gather,
The melancholy unconsoling fold
Of all things that go utterly to death
And mix no more, no more
With life's perpetually awakening breath?
Shall Time not ferry me to such a shore,
Over such sailless seas,

To walk with hope's slain importunities
In miserable marriage? Nay, shall not
All things be there forgot,
Save the sea's golden barrier and the black
Close-crouching promontories?
Dead to all shames, forgotten of all glories,
Shall I not wander there, a shadow's shade,
A spectre self-destroyed,
So purged of all remembrance and sucked back
Into the primal void,
That should we on that shore phantasmal meet
I should not know the coming of your feet?

Growing Old by Matthew Arnold

What is it to grow old?
Is it to lose the glory of the form,

The lustre of the eye?
Is it for beauty to forego her wreath?
Yes, but not for this alone.

Is it to feel our strength—
Not our bloom only, but our strength—decay?
Is it to feel each limb
Grow stiffer, every function less exact,
Each nerve more weakly strung?

Yes, this, and more! but not,
Ah, 'tis not what in youth we dreamed 'twould be!
'Tis not to have our life
Mellowed and softened as with sunset-glow,
A golden day's decline!

'Tis not to see the world
As from a height, with rapt prophetic eyes,
And heart profoundly stirred;
And weep, and feel the fulness of the past,
The years that are no more!

It is to spend long days
And not once feel that we were ever young.

It is to add, immured
In the hot prison of the present, month
To month with weary pain.

It is to suffer this,
And feel but half, and feebly, what we feel:
Deep in our hidden heart
Festers the dull remembrance of a change,
But no emotion—none.

It is—last stage of all—
When we are frozen up within, and quite
The phantom of ourselves,
To hear the world applaud the hollow ghost
Which blamed the living man.

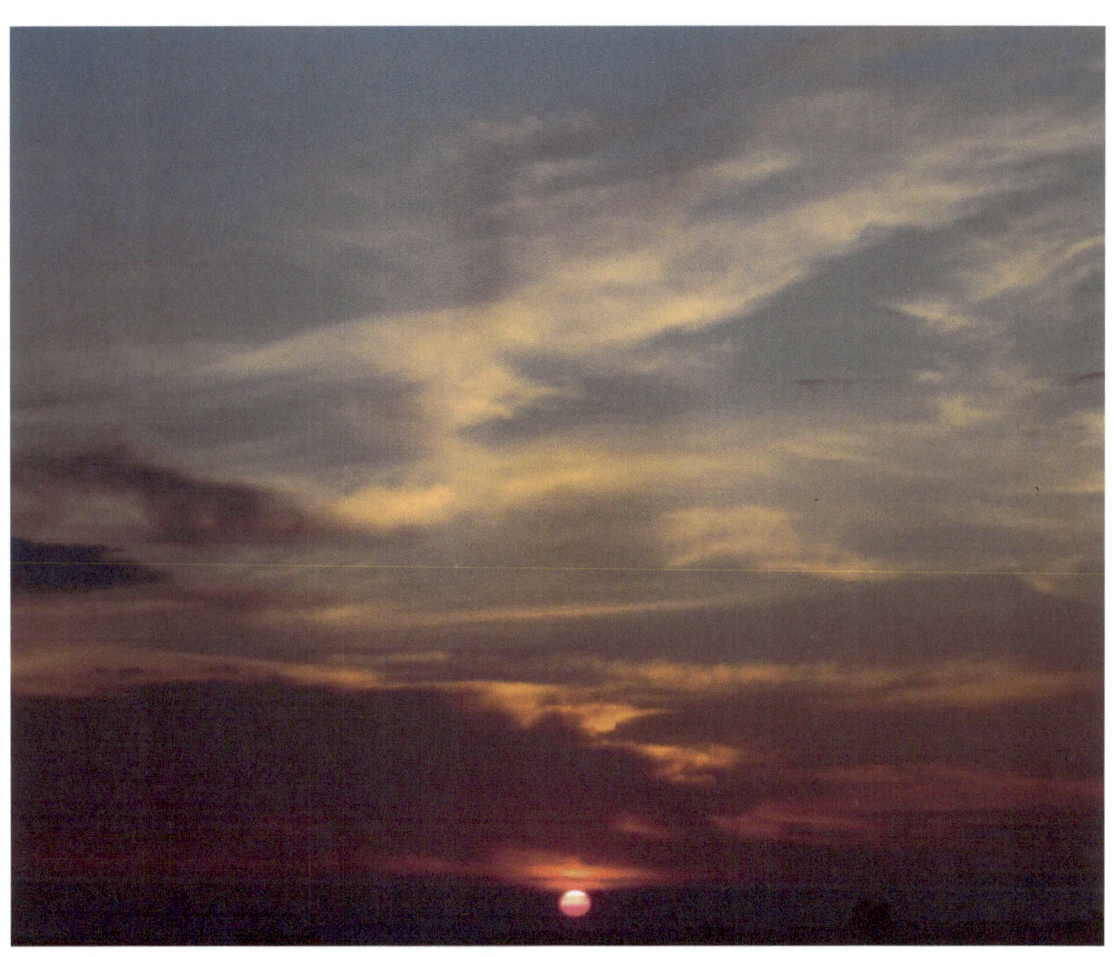

A Peck of Gold by Robert Frost

Dust always blowing about the town,
Except when sea-fog laid it down,
And I was one of the children told
Some of the blowing dust was gold.

All the dust the wind blew high
Appeared like god in the sunset sky,
But I was one of the children told
Some of the dust was really gold.

Such was life in the Golden Gate:
Gold dusted all we drank and ate,

And I was one of the children told,
'We all must eat our peck of gold.
'

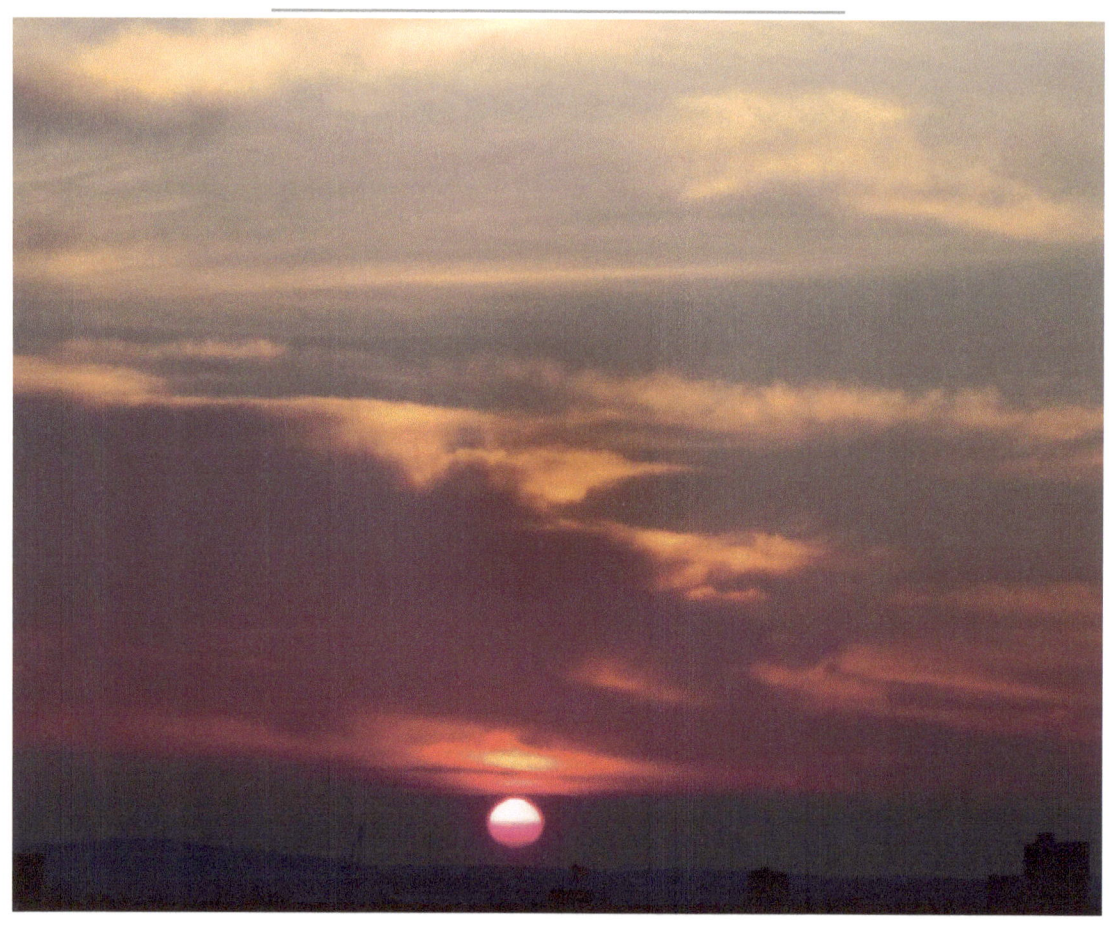

From Sunset to Star Rise by Christina Rossetti

Go from me, summer friends, and tarry not:
I am no summer friend, but wintry cold,
A silly sheep benighted from the fold,
A sluggard with a thorn-choked garden plot.

Take counsel, sever from my lot your lot,
Dwell in your pleasant places, hoard your gold;
Lest you with me should shiver on the wold,
Athirst and hungering on a barren spot.

For I have hedged me with a thorny hedge,
I live alone, I look to die alone:
Yet sometimes, when a wind sighs through the sedge,
Ghosts of my buried years, and friends come back,
My heart goes sighing after swallows flown
On sometime summer's unreturning track.

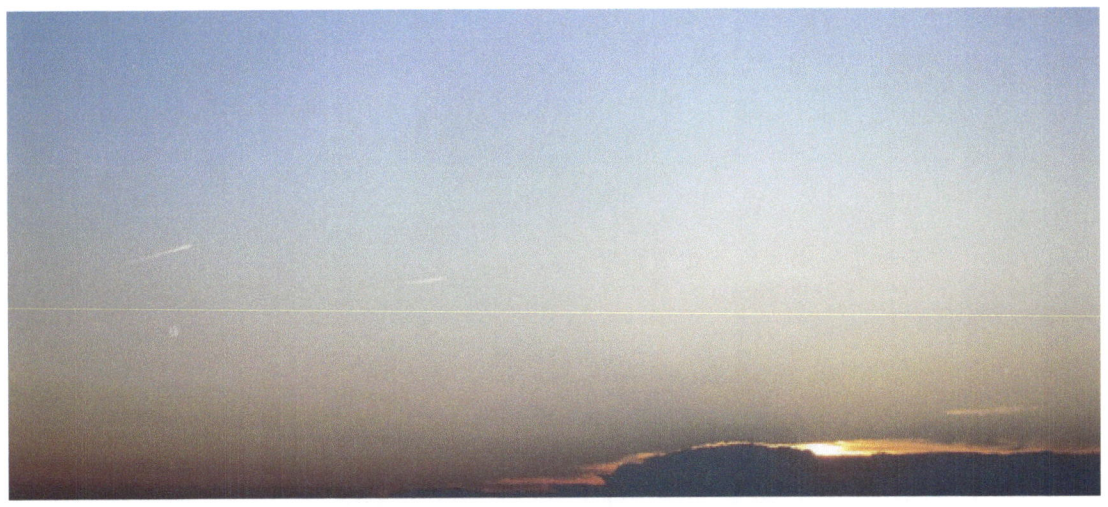

An ignorance a Sunset by Emily Dickinson

An ignorance a Sunset
Confer upon the Eye --
Of Territory -- Color --
Circumference -- Decay --

Its Amber Revelation
Exhilirate -- Debase --
Omnipotence' inspection
Of Our inferior face --

And when the solemn features
Confirm -- in Victory --
We start -- as if detected
In Immortality --

Autumn Song by Sarojini Naidu

Like a joy on the heart of a sorrow,
 The sunset hangs on a cloud;
A golden storm of glittering sheaves,
Of fair and frail and fluttering leaves,
 The wild wind blows in a cloud.

Hark to a voice that is calling
 To my heart in the voice of the wind:
My heart is weary and sad and alone,
For its dreams like the fluttering leaves have gone,
 And why should I stay behind?

An April Day by Henry Wadsworth Longfellow

 When the warm sun, that brings
Seed-time and harvest, has returned again,
'T is sweet to visit the still wood, where springs
The first flower of the plain.

I love the season well,
When forest glades are teeming with bright forms,
Nor dark and many-folded clouds foretell
The coming-on of storms.

From the earth's loosened mould
The sapling draws its sustenance, and thrives;
Though stricken to the heart with winter's cold,
The drooping tree revives.

The softly-warbled song
Comes from the pleasant woods, and colored wings
Glance quick in the bright sun, that moves along
The forest openings.

When the bright sunset fills
The silver woods with light, the green slope throws
Its shadows in the hollows of the hills,
And wide the upland glows.

And when the eve is born,
In the blue lake the sky, o'er-reaching far,
Is hollowed out and the moon dips her horn,
And twinkles many a star.

Inverted in the tide
Stand the gray rocks, and trembling shadows throw,
And the fair trees look over, side by side,
And see themselves below.

Sweet April! many a thought
Is wedded unto thee, as hearts are wed;
Nor shall they fail, till, to its autumn brought,
Life's golden fruit is shed.

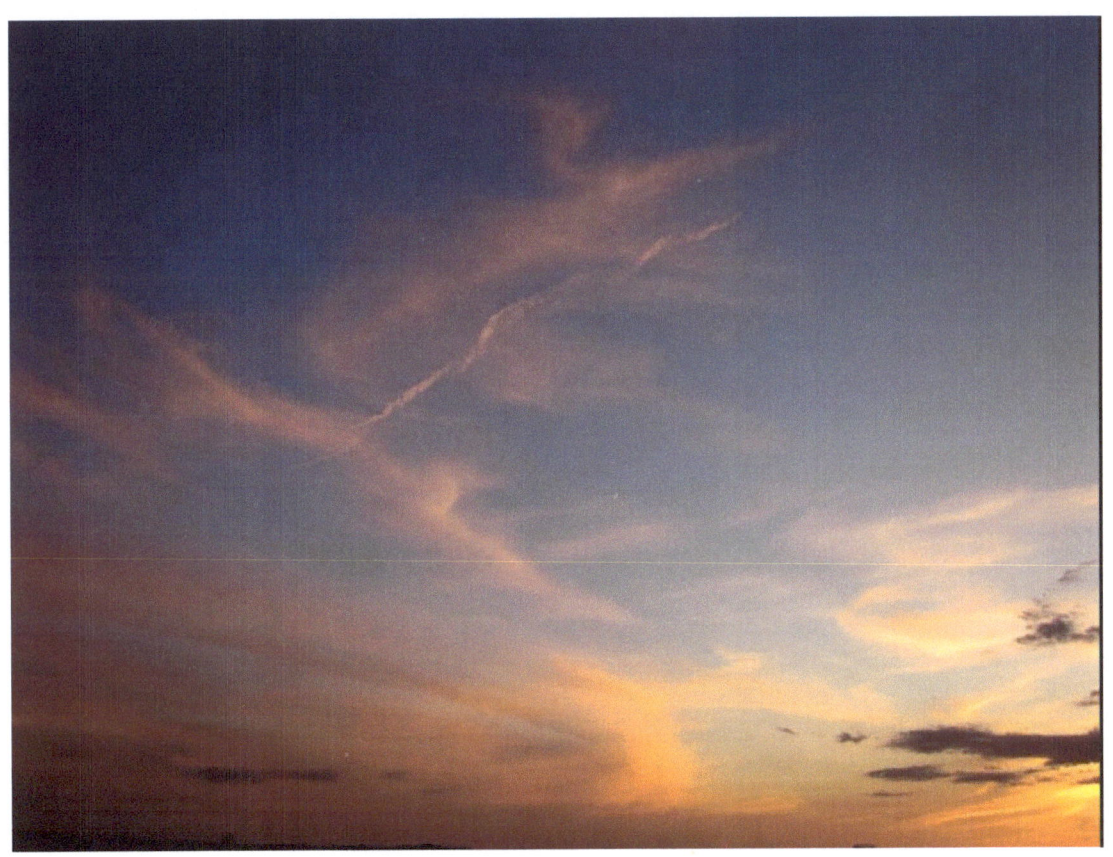

The Black Birds by Henry Van Dyke

I

Once, only once, I saw it clear, --
That Eden every human heart has dreamed
A hundred times, but always far away!
Ah, well do I remember how it seemed,
Through the still atmosphere
Of that enchanted day,
To lie wide open to my weary feet:
A little land of love and joy and rest,
With meadows of soft green,
Rosy with cyclamen, and sweet
With delicate breath of violets unseen, --
And, tranquil 'mid the bloom
As if it waited for a coming guest,
A little house of peace and joy and love
Was nested like a snow-white dove

From the rough mountain where I stood,
Homesick for happiness,
Only a narrow valley and a darkling wood
To cross, and then the long distress
Of solitude would be forever past, --
I should be home at last.

But not too soon! oh, let me linger here
And feed my eyes, hungry with sorrow,
On all this loveliness, so near,
And mine to-morrow!

Then, from the wood, across the silvery blue,
A dark bird flew,
Silent, with sable wings.

Close in his wake another came, --
Fragments of midnight floating through
The sunset flame, --
Another and another, weaving rings
Of blackness on the primrose sky, --
Another, and another, look, a score,
A hundred, yes, a thousand rising heavily
From that accursed, dumb, and ancient wood, --
They boiled into the lucid air
Like smoke from some deep caldron of despair!
And more, and more, and ever more,
The numberless, ill-omened brood,
Flapping their ragged plumes,
Possessed the landscape and the evening light
With menaces and glooms.

Oh, dark, dark, dark they hovered o'er the place
Where once I saw the little house so white
Amid the flowers, covering every trace
Of beauty from my troubled sight, --
And suddenly it was night!

II

At break of day I crossed the wooded vale;
And while the morning made
A trembling light among the tree-tops pale,
I saw the sable birds on every limb,
Clinging together closely in the shade,
And croaking placidly their surly hymn.

But, oh, the little land of peace and love
That those night-loving wings had poised above, --
Where was it gone?
Lost, lost forevermore!
Only a cottage, dull and gray,
In the cold light of dawn,
With iron bars across the door:
Only a garden where the withering heads
Of flowers, presaging decay,
Hung over barren beds:
Only a desolate field that lay
Untilled beneath the desolate day, --
Where Eden seemed to bloom I found but these!
So, wondering, I passed along my way,
With anger in my heart, too deep for words,
Against that grove of evil-sheltering trees,
And the black magic of the croaking birds.

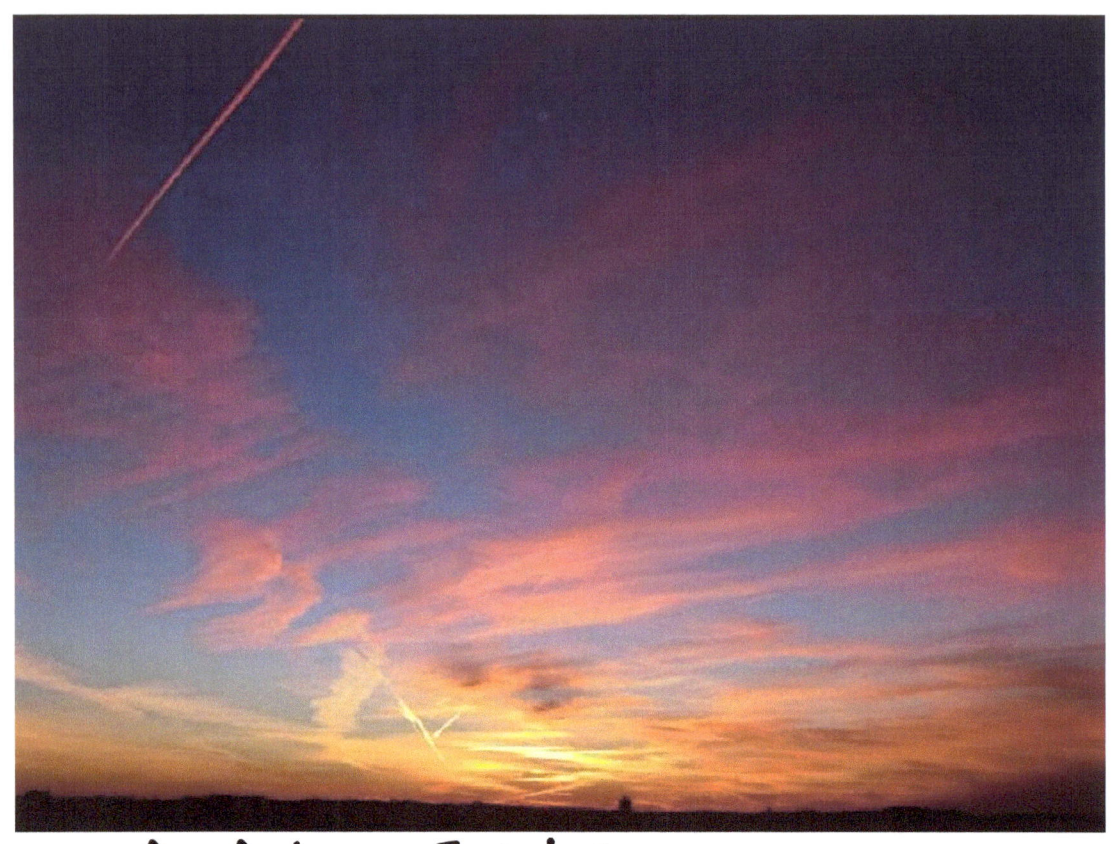

An Autumn Evening by Lucy Maud Montgomery

Dark hills against a hollow crocus sky
Scarfed with its crimson pennons, and below
The dome of sunset long, hushed valleys lie
Cradling the twilight, where the lone winds blow
And wake among the harps of leafless trees
Fantastic runes and mournful melodies.

The chilly purple air is threaded through
With silver from the rising moon afar,
And from a gulf of clear, unfathomed blue
In the southwest glimmers a great gold star
Above the darkening druid glens of fir
Where beckoning boughs and elfin voices stir.

And so I wander through the shadows still,
And look and listen with a rapt delight,
Pausing again and yet again at will

To drink the elusive beauty of the night,
Until my soul is filled, as some deep cup,
That with divine enchantment is brimmed up.

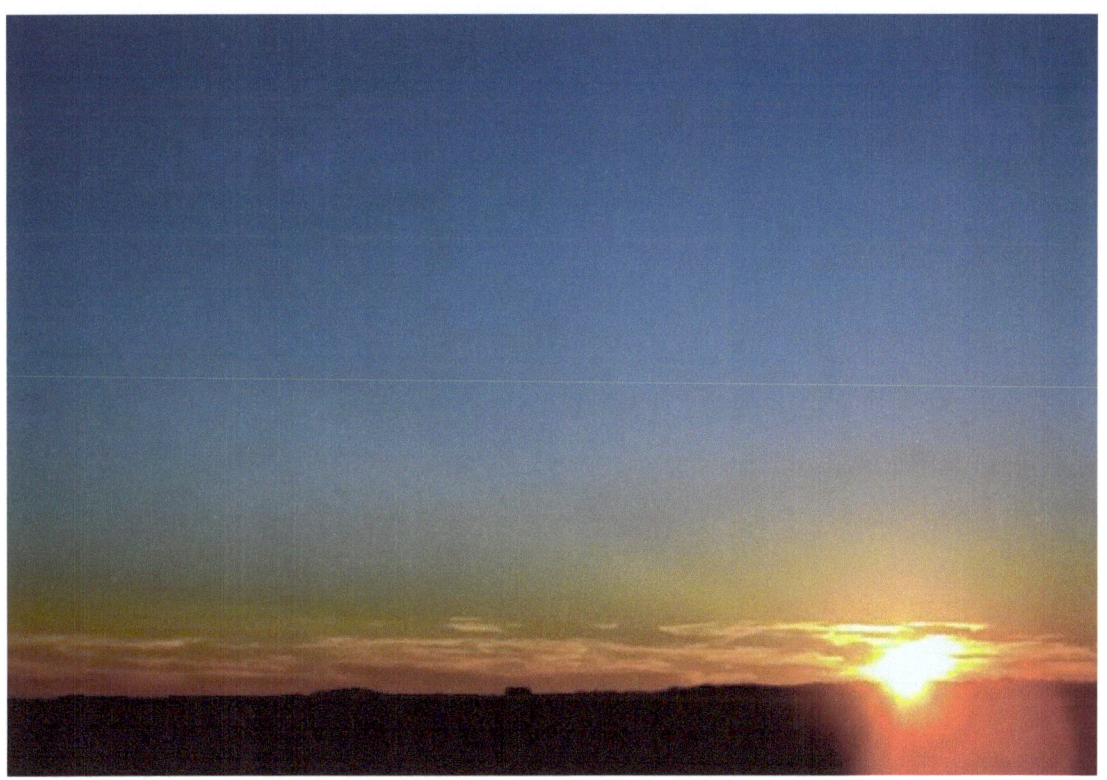

The New Colossus by Emma Lazarus

Not like the brazen giant of Greek fame,
With conquering limbs astride from land to land;
Here at our sea-washed, sunset gates shall stand
A mighty woman with a torch, whose flame
Is the imprisoned lightning, and her name
Mother of Exiles.
   From her beacon-hand
Glows world-wide welcome; her mild eyes command
The air-bridged harbor that twin cities frame.

"Keep, ancient lands, your storied pomp!" cries she
With silent lips.
   "Give me your tired, your poor,
Your huddled masses yearning to breathe free,

The wretched refuse of your teeming shore.

Send these, the homeless, tempest-tost to me,
I lift my lamp beside the golden door!"

Crossing the Bar by Alfred Lord Tennyson

Sunset and evening star,
And one clear call for me!
And may there be no moaning of the bar,
When I put out to sea,

But such a tide as moving seems asleep,

Too full for sound and foam,
When that which drew from out the boundless deep
Turns again home.

Twilight and evening bell,
And after that the dark!
And may there be no sadness of farewell,
When I embark;

For though from out our bourne of Time and Place
The flood may bear me far,
I hope to see my Pilot face to face
When I have crossed the bar.

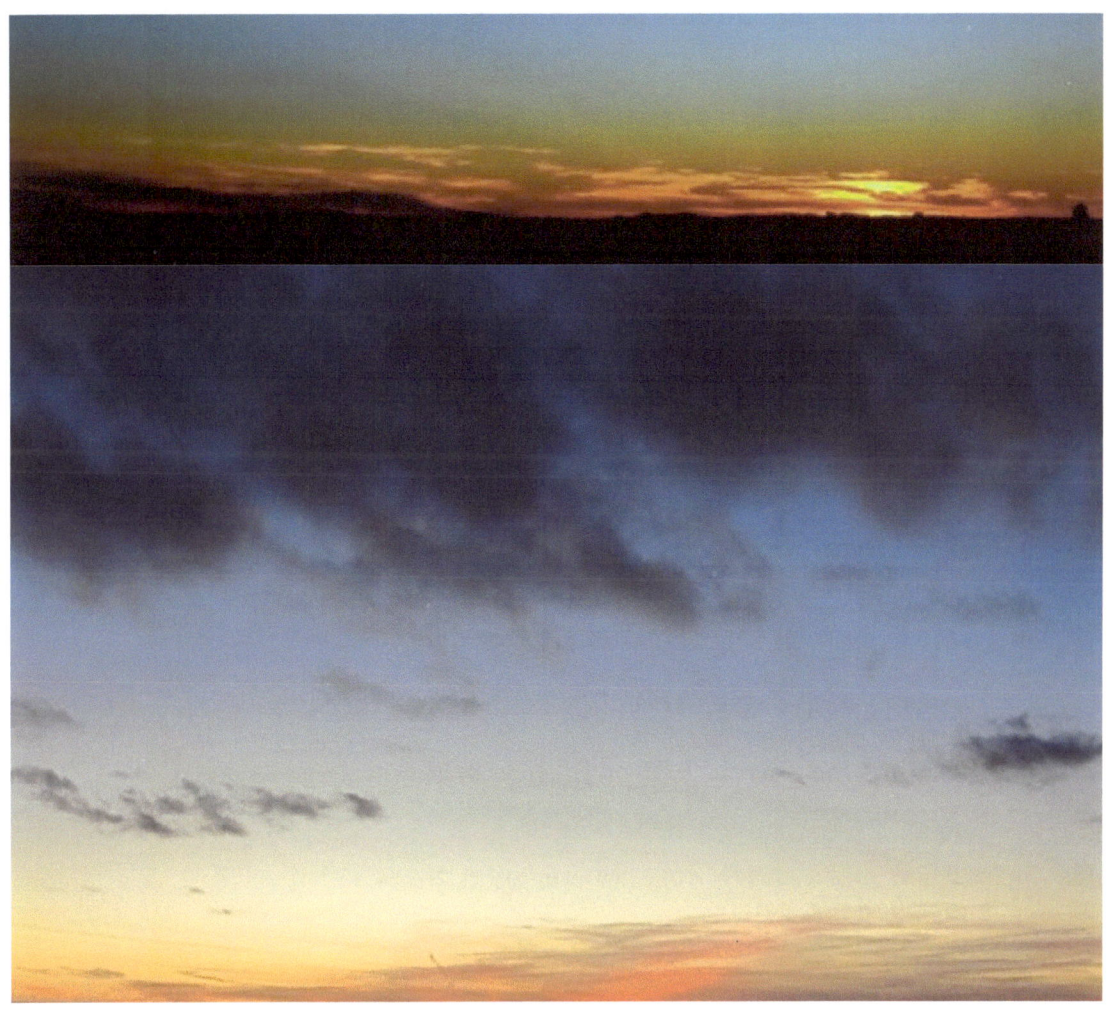

A Sunset of the City by Gwendolyn Brooks

Already I am no longer looked at with lechery or love.

My daughters and sons have put me away with marbles and dolls,
Are gone from the house.

My husband and lovers are pleasant or somewhat polite
And night is night.

It is a real chill out,
The genuine thing.

I am not deceived, I do not think it is still summer
Because sun stays and birds continue to sing.

It is summer-gone that I see, it is summer-gone.

The sweet flowers in drying and dying down,
The grasses forgetting their blaze and consenting to brown.

It is a real chill out.
  The fall crisp comes
I am aware there is winter to heed.

There is no warm house
That is fitted with my need.

I am cold in this cold house this house
Whose washed echoes are tremulous down lost halls.

I am a woman, and dusty, standing among new affairs.

I am a woman who hurries through her prayers.

Tin intimations of a quiet core to be my
Desert and my dear relief
Come: there shall be such islanding from grief,

And small communion with the master shore.

Twang they.
 And I incline this ear to tin,
Consult a dual dilemma.
 Whether to dry
In humming pallor or to leap and die.

Somebody muffed it?? Somebody wanted to joke

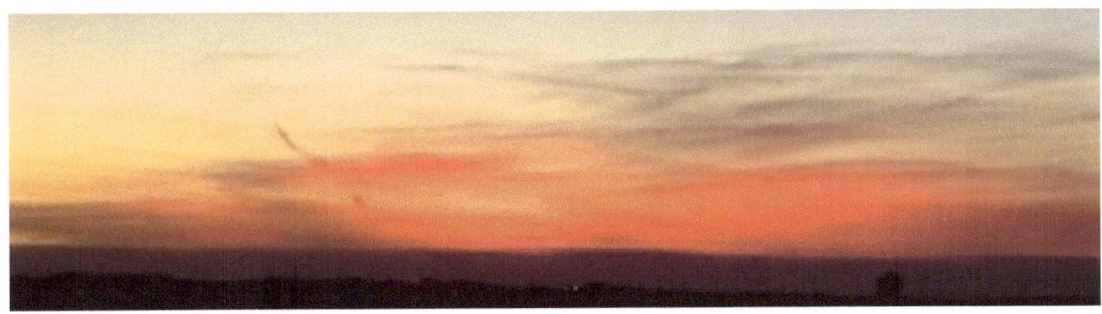

First Fig by Edna St. Vincent Millay

My candle burns at both ends;
It will not last the night;
But ah, my foes, and oh, my friends—
It gives a lovely light.

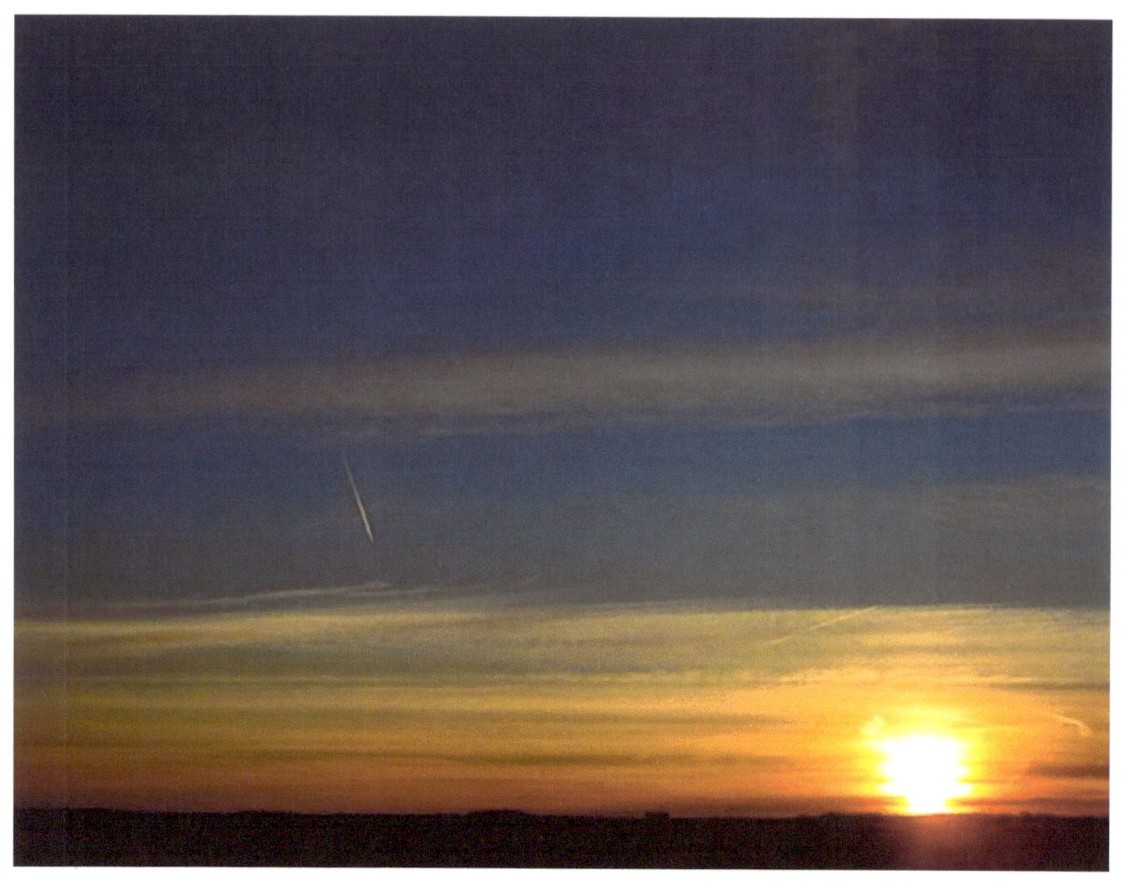

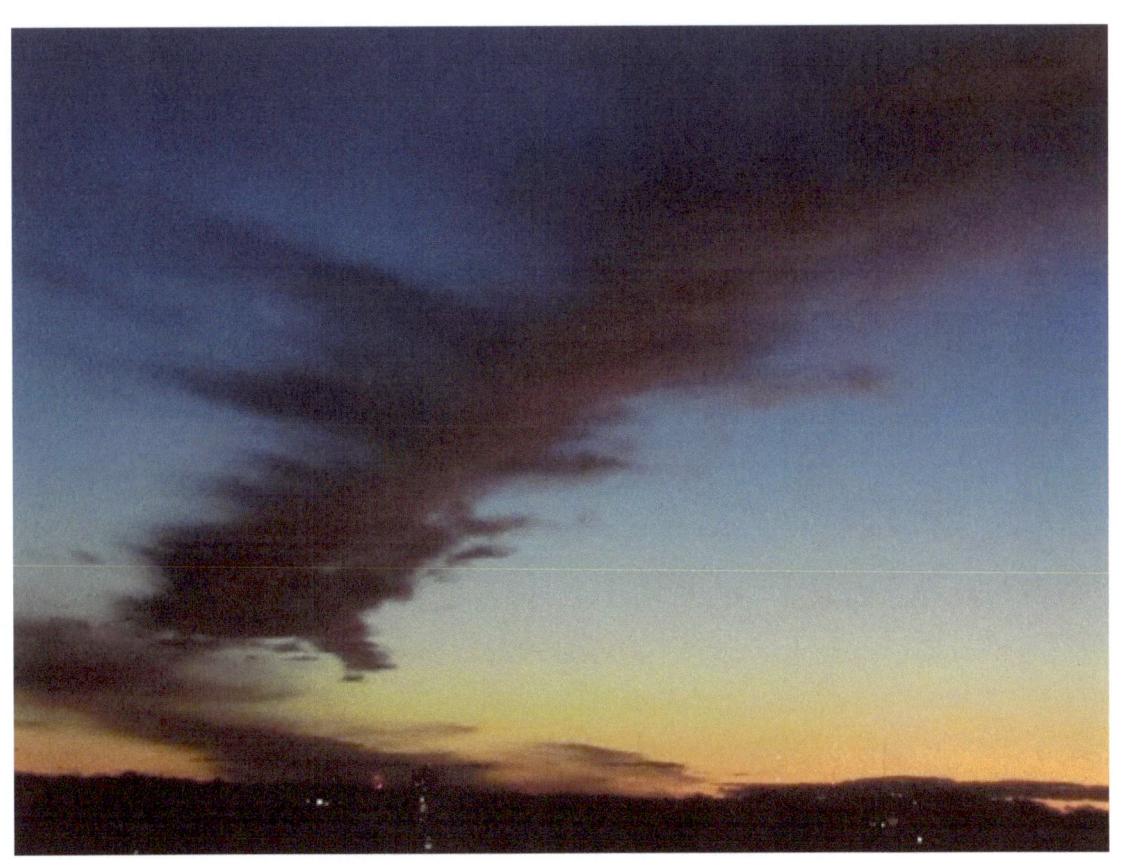

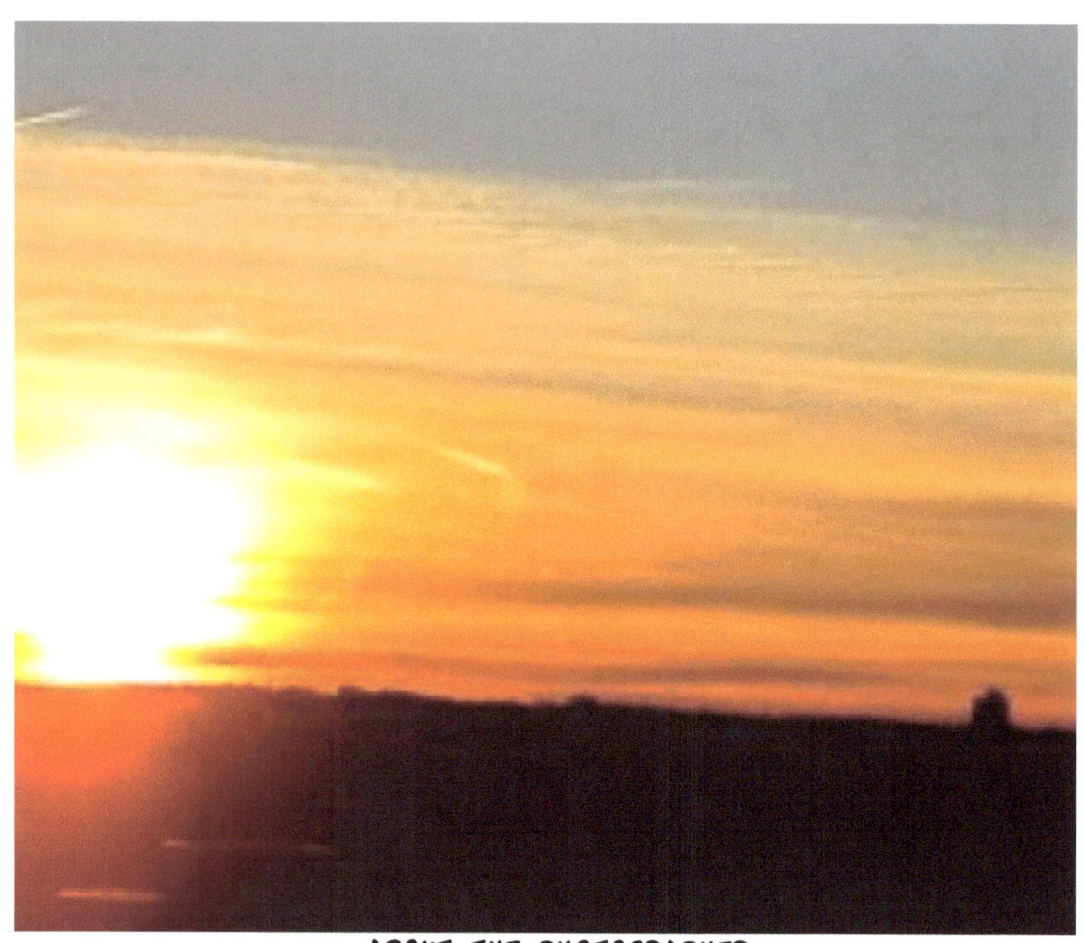

ABOUT THE PHOTOGRAPHER

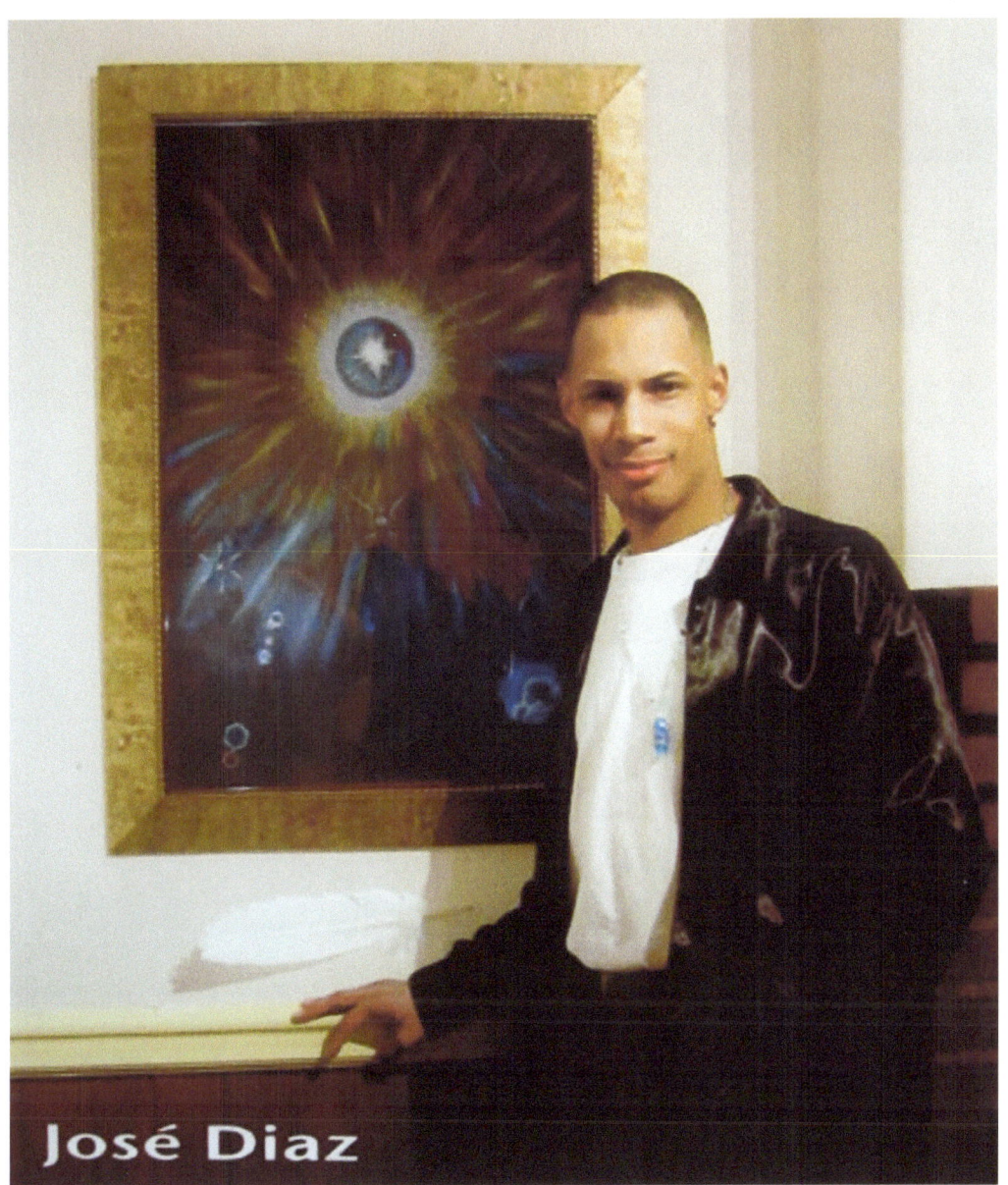

José Diaz

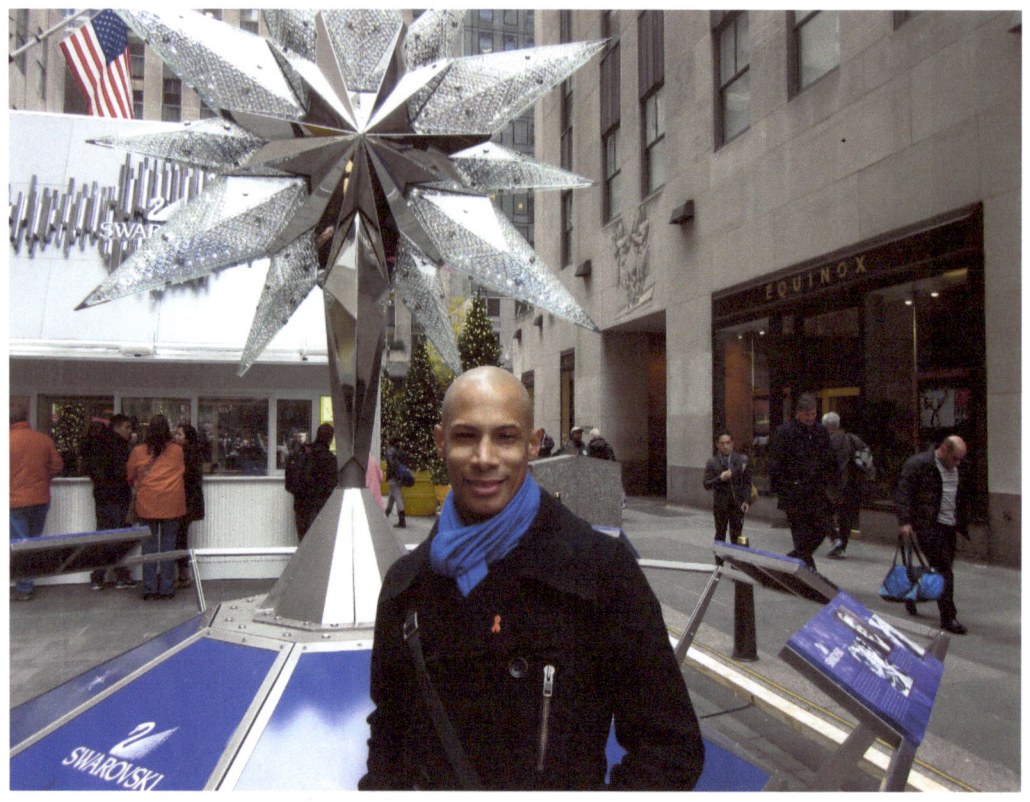

Artist Jose Diaz in Manhattan, 2012

ART WORK INCLUDED IN THIS VOLUME MAY BE
PURCHASED FROM JOSE DIAZ.

YOU MAY REACH MR. DIAZ AT jdiaz5272@gmail.com
FOR FURTHER INFORMATION.

*The artist would like to thank collectors of his art for their support
and for giving permission to include his work in this volume.*

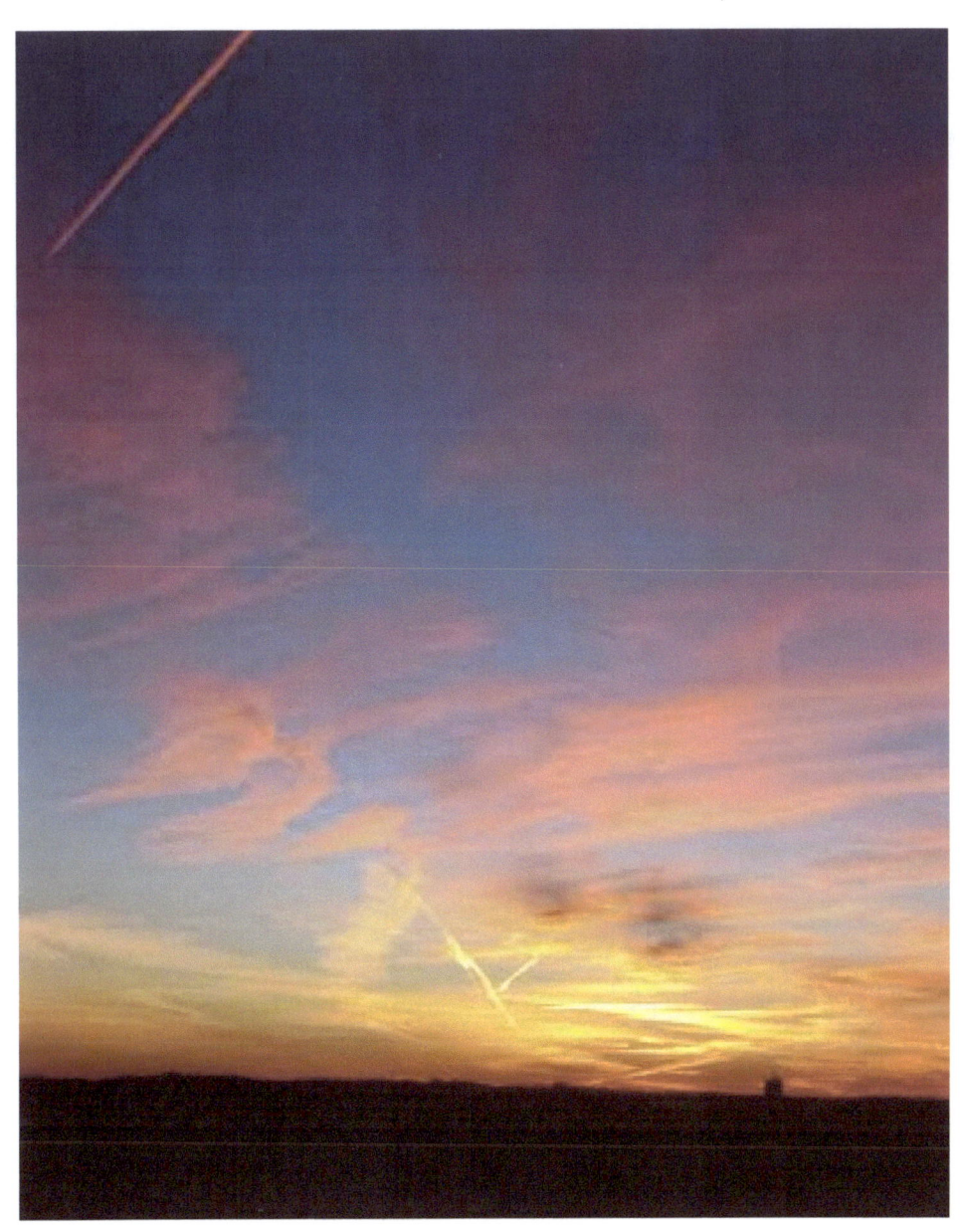

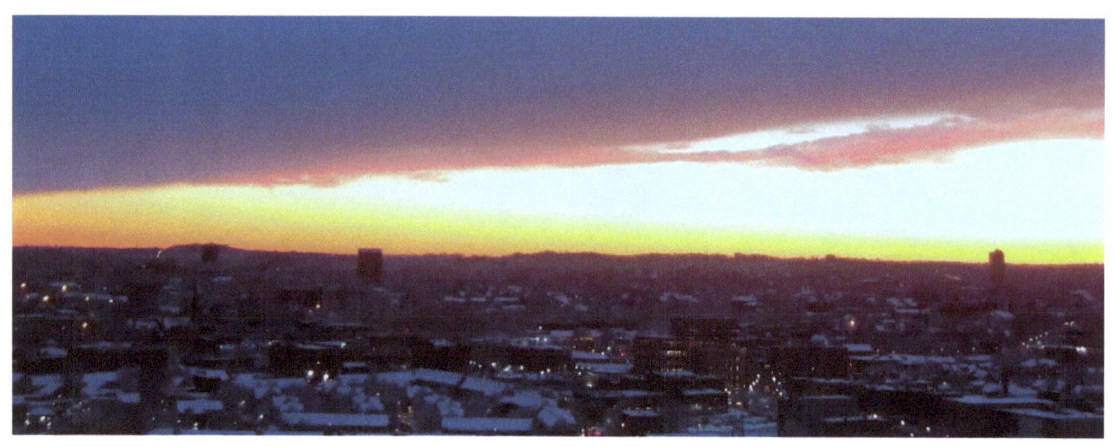

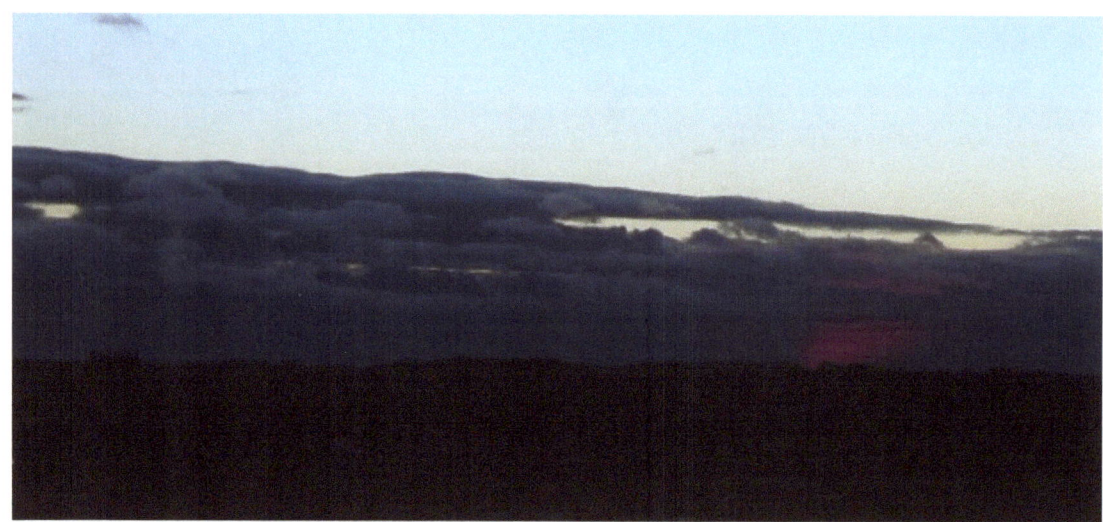